Who Likes the Night?

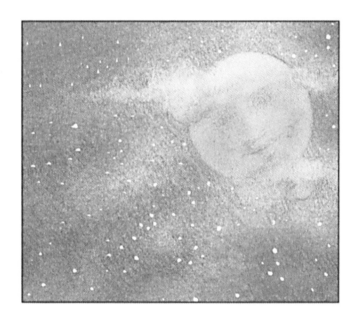

Anna Kunari
Illustrations by Linda Graves

HAMPTON-BROWN

Who likes the night? Moon likes the night. Moon gets up when the sun goes down.

Moon up high
like a pie in the sky,
what would night be
without you?

Who likes the night? Star likes the night. Star gets up when the sun goes down.

Star up high
like a light in the sky,
moon up high
like a pie in the sky,
what would night be
without you?

Who likes the night? Owl likes the night. Owl gets up when the sun goes down.

Owl up high
in a tree watching me,
star up high
like a light in the sky,
moon up high
like a pie in the sky,
what would night be
without you?

Who likes the night? Fox likes the night. Fox gets up when the sun goes down.

Fox up high
so still on the hill,
owl up high
in a tree watching me,
star up high
like a light in the sky,
moon up high
like a pie in the sky,
what would night be
without you?

Who likes the night? Moth likes the night. Moth gets up when the sun goes down.

Moth up high
in the bright moonlight,
fox up high
so still on the hill,
owl up high
in a tree watching me,
star up high
like a light in the sky,
moon up high
like a pie in the sky,
what would night be
without you?

Who likes the night?
I like the night.

And I like the moth
in the moonlight,
the fox on the hill,
the owl in the tree,
and the star and the moon
in the sky.
I like them all,
but nighttime is bedtime for me.

So, good night, my friends.
Good night!